POTATOES

A COUNTRY GARDEN COOKBOOK

POTATOES

A COUNTRY GARDEN COOKBOOK

By Maggie Waldron

Photography by Deborah Jones

CollinsPublishersSanFrancisco

A Division of HarperCollinsPublishers

First published in the USA in 1993 by Collins Publishers San Francisco
Copyright © 1993 Collins Publishers San Francisco
Recipes and text copyright © 1993 Maggie Waldron
Photographs copyright © 1993 Deborah Jones
Food Stylist: Sandra Cook
Floral and Prop Stylist: Michaele Thunen
Project Direction, Art Direction and Design: Jennifer Barry
Editor: Meesha Halm
Library of Congress Cataloging-in-Publication Data:
Waldron, Maggie
Potatoes: a country garden cookbook/recipes by Maggie Waldron:
photography by Deborah Jones.
p. cm.
Includes index.
ISBN 0-00-255226-4
1. Cookery (Potatoes)   I. Title.
TX803.P8SW35   1993
641.6'521--dc20   CIP 93-7418
Printed in China   10 9 8 7 6 5 4 3 2

CONTENTS

INTRODUCTION

If you don't have space for a country garden, take a tip from a friend of mine who surmised that in this world there are 30 billion discarded tires with no place to go. He suggests you plant potatoes in them, as they do in developing countries. You can do this wherever you live, even if it is a crowded city or a desert. The tires retain moisture after watering so the seedlings are not in danger of drying up. The potato growers even paint the tires pretty pastel colors to go with their houses. What a nice idea!

One of the most fascinating men on any subject, but particularly on potatoes, is the 1990 Laureate of the World Food Prize, Dr. John S. Niederhauser. He won this international award for his work in alleviating world hunger and malnutrition based on the humble spud. And since potatoes are my pet subject, having worked with The Potato Board for some fifteen years to help some 12,000 potato farmers sell their crops, I feel a special kinship with Dr. Niederhauser. And this little book.

Although the potato has had some hard knocks along the way, it is without a doubt the world's favorite vegetable. Vegetable? Yes, although it was designated as a starch for many years before people learned how nutritionally rich it really was. I once had the nerve to paint a potato bright green for an educational pamphlet that read, "How far do we have to go before you think of us as a vegetable?"

Potatoes have lots of vitamin C and fiber, two nutritional elements recognized as cancer fighters by the American Cancer Society. The fiber in potato skins also helps lower blood cholesterol, which is good news for your heart. The high potassium content can reduce blood pressure and, along with it, the risk of stroke. In addition, potatoes are low in calories, which is good news for those wrestling with their weight, as long as they steer clear of the butter, sour cream and bacon bits. The British believed that potatoes could be used to ease rheumatism—not by eating them, however, but by carrying one around in your pocket.

Bake them, boil them, cook them in a microwave or roast them over the coals—potatoes seem the most versatile and undemanding of vegetables. However, this most unprepossessing tuber is not as innocent as one might be led to believe. The potato has seen a lot of action over the centuries. It was said to have been fertilized with human blood by the Incas and provided the only form of sustenance for thousands of prisoners and civilians in both world wars.

Every old wife had a tale about sowing seeds with a waxing, never a waning, moon. Scientists finally caught up, having discovered the effects of lunar rhythms on the earth's magnetic field, which in turn affects growth. They have established that all water everywhere, including that inside the tiniest living organism, moves in tides like the sea. The moon affects the earth's atmosphere so that it is more likely to rain heavily immediately after a full or new moon. Apparently, a potato grown at constant levels of heat and light under laboratory conditions will still show a growth rhythm that reflects the lunar pattern. The old wife, without laboratory conditions or statistical tables, knew how to get her plants off to a good start.

In this age of designer potatoes, you can choose your color, flavor, texture and nationality. Try them all. You will soon discover the many personas of the potato.

GLOSSARY

Varieties: Our gardening grandfathers would get a laugh out of the latest potato fashions. Organic farmers and independent growers are reintroducing some of the old-time varieties that aren't mass-marketed as are the four leaders in the field: the russet, the long white, the round white and the round red. Generally, the uses of potatoes vary according to starch content. Russets have high starch content and a mealy texture, which makes them an ideal baking potato and a good choice for mashed potatoes. Those with medium starch are most suitable for an all-purpose potato. The small reds or "new" potatoes are low in starch because they are harvested before reaching maturity. These are waxy in texture and work best in salads.

Selection: Potatoes should be fairly clean, firm and smooth. Avoid potatoes that are wrinkled, have wilted skins, soft dark areas, cut surfaces or a green appearance. Choose potatoes with regular, uniform shapes so that there won't be too much waste in peeling and so that they will cook evenly.

Storing: Store potatoes in a cool, humid (but not wet), dark place that is well ventilated, approximately 45 to 50 degrees F. At this temperature, potatoes will keep for several weeks. Warmer temperatures encourage sprouting and shriveling. Avoid prolonged exposure to light, which causes potatoes to turn green. This green causes a bitter flavor and should be pared away before the potato is used. Sprouting potatoes can still be used. Just break off the sprouts and peel before cooking. Do not refrigerate potatoes. Refrigeration causes the potatoes to develop a sweet taste and to turn brown when fried.

Equivalents: One pound of potatoes equals:
3 medium potatoes
10 small potatoes
3 cups potatoes, peeled and sliced
2 1/4 cups potatoes, peeled and diced
2 cups mashed potatoes
2 cups french fries

High-Starch Potatoes:

Russet: Varieties include Arcadia, Burbank and Idaho. Oval-shaped, with brown skin and white flesh. Their high starch content and mealy texture make them an ideal baking potato and a good choice for mashed potatoes.

Medium-Starch Potatoes:

Long White (also called White Rose or New White): Oval-shaped, light tan skin with white flesh; an ideal all-purpose potato.

Peruvian Blue: Oval-shaped, dark blue skin with deep purple flesh; approximately the same size as the russet; an all-purpose potato.

Round White (also called Eastern Potato): Varieties include California, Canada, Chippewa, Delaware, Irish Cobbler, Katahdin, Kennebec, Long Island, Maine and Superior. Round-shaped, light tan skin with white flesh; an all-purpose potato, ideal scalloped, roasted and cut into salads.

Yellow Finnish (also called Yellow Finn): Round-shaped, tan skin with pale yellow flesh; one of the newest potatoes on the block. With its creamy texture and golden color, it can fool you into thinking that it is buttered.

Yukon Gold: Round-shaped, light tan skin with deep-yellow flesh; makes the creamiest mashed potatoes ever, but you will be surprised how good they are baked and French fried. Also comes in a smaller, baby variety.

Low-Starch Potatoes:

Fingerling: Varieties include Ruby Crescent and Russian fingerling. Pink, yellow, blue or light beige skins with similarly colored flesh; these potatoes are approximately 3 inches long and 1 inch wide, giving them their fingerlike shape. Ideal steamed, roasted or barbecued.

Round Red: Varieties include La Soda, La Touge, Red Norland and Red Pontiac. Round-shaped, red skins with white flesh. Small reds, often called New Potatoes, are harvested before they reach maturity in the late spring and last throughout the summer. When picked at a young age, they are low in starch and sweet in flavor, making them a poor choice for baking but ideal for roasting and frying. They are waxy in texture and also work well sliced or diced in potato salads. (When you see them in the market in the dead of winter, you know that they have been held in cold storage.) When harvested later in the season, red potatoes grow to full size with a higher starch content.

Growing: Would you like to grow potatoes without getting your hands dirty? Then grow what the English call straw potatoes. Fill a barrel with old straw and stuff some cut-up potatoes in the middle with the eyes looking up. Cover with a shallow layer of straw and water every week to ten days. Be patient for approximately three weeks, then peek under the straw. Voila! You should have whole potatoes, if Mother Nature cooperates.

The small seed potatoes should arrive early in the new year. Spread them out on egg trays in a cool, light place for four to six weeks until they have produced short shoots. Potatoes like an acid soil that is mixed with plenty of well-rotted compost. Good Friday is the preferred day for planting taters in England, but any day in early spring will do fine. Follow directions from the supplier of the small seed potatoes for planting the sprouted potatoes in rows, covered with a layer of soil. As soon as the shoots appear above the soil, cover them with another layer of soil; approximately a month later, cover with another layer of soil. When the plants come into flower, the potatoes, in all of their glory, are ready. Steam them until tender, and serve them with butter and a little chopped parsley or mint as a course all by themselves, the pièce de résistance.

Fingerlings (Ruby Crescents)

Round White

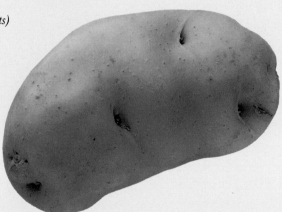

Long White (White Rose)

Round Red

Small Red

Baby Yukon Gold

Yukon Gold

Yellow Finnish

Russet

Peruvian Blue

OPENERS

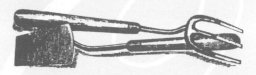

You rarely see potatoes listed under "openers," but this is one of my favorite ways to use them. Start with a nourishing soup made with potatoes as the background and almost any tasty seasonal vegetable as the foreground. With a sprightly salad or a sandwich, you can call almost any potato soup a meal.

The hot wheels with varying degrees of heat can be rolled out with the predinner drinks as can the simple little crispy Dutch new potatoes with herbs and bread crumbs. For something more substantial, string potato chunks seasoned with rosemary on skewers and slip them on the grill or under the broiler. For a little razzle-dazzle, pasilla peppers stuffed with potatoes and cheese, pumpkin-potato ravioli, potato hummus with pita chips or a colorful antipasto all fit the bill as enticing first courses. A refreshing green salad with lots of herbs topped with little fried potato croutons is one of my favorite ways to get a dinner moving merrily along.

Leek, Potato and Spinach Soup

Although starchy russets add substance to this earthy garden soup, you might want to try round whites for potatoes with a firmer texture. Yukon Golds or round reds add a festive color.

1/4 cup salted butter or margarine
4 cups water
1 cup thinly sliced leeks
1 1/2 pounds potatoes (4 to 5 medium),
    sliced 1/4 inch thick

6 cups coarsely chopped spinach
Salt and freshly ground black pepper to taste
Sour cream

In a 3-quart saucepan over high heat, melt the butter in 1 cup of the water. Add leeks, cover and simmer over low heat for 5 minutes. Add the potatoes and the remaining water; bring to boil and cook until potatoes are tender, approximately 15 minutes.

Just before serving, add the spinach and simmer gently for 5 minutes. Season with salt and pepper. Serve hot, garnished with a swirl of sour cream. *Serves 4 to 6*

Potato-Cheese Soup, Hot or Not

Russet, White Rose or Yukon Gold potatoes would be most suitable for their creamy texture in this tangy buttermilk soup. Yukon Golds give it a sunny color.

1 1/3 pounds potatoes (4 medium),
  peeled and thinly sliced
1 medium leek (white portion only),
  thinly sliced
2 1/2 cups chicken stock,
  homemade or low-sodium canned

1 cup water
1 1/2 cups buttermilk
1 cup shredded Asiago cheese
Freshly ground black pepper to taste
Chopped parsley and thinly sliced green onions,
  for garnish

In a 2-quart saucepan, combine the potatoes, leek, stock and water. Bring to boil; cover and cook until potatoes are tender, approximately 10 minutes. Transfer to an electric blender or food processor and blend until almost smooth.

Return the soup to the saucepan. Stir in the buttermilk. Bring to a simmer. Gradually add the cheese, stirring constantly until the cheese melts. Season with pepper. Serve hot, or cover and chill for several hours to serve cool. Garnish each serving with a sprinkle of parsley and green onions. *Serves 4 to 6*

Butternut Squash and Potato Soup

Liquid gold and velvety smooth, this soup is creamy without the addition of cream.
Finish it with a swirl of emerald green pesto.

1 pound russet potatoes (3 medium), peeled
    and cut into 1-inch chunks
1 pound butternut squash, peeled, seeded and
    cut into 1-inch chunks
1/2 cup thinly sliced onion
2 3/4 cups chicken stock, homemade or
    low-sodium canned
1 cup lowfat milk
1 1/2 tablespoons fresh lemon juice
1 teaspoon salt, or to taste
1/4 teaspoon hot pepper sauce, or to taste

Pesto:
1 cup fresh basil leaves, tightly packed in
    a measuring cup
1/4 cup olive oil
1 tablespoon pine nuts
1 clove garlic, crushed
1/2 teaspoon salt
1/4 cup freshly grated Parmesan cheese
1 tablespoon freshly grated
    Pecorino Romano cheese
1 1/2 tablespoons salted butter, softened

In a heavy saucepan, combine the potatoes, squash, onion and stock. Bring to a boil, cover and cook until vegetables are tender, approximately 15 minutes. Transfer to an electric blender or food processor and add milk. Blend or process until smooth.

Return the soup to the saucepan. Season with lemon juice, salt and pepper sauce. (If the soup seems too thick, thin it down with a small amount of water or milk.) Gently bring to a boil, stirring constantly.

Prepare the pesto: Put the basil leaves, olive oil, pine nuts, garlic and salt in a food processor and process at high speed until you have a smooth purée. Transfer into a bowl and stir in the cheeses and butter. Add 2 tablespoons of boiling water just before serving to thin the sauce and melt the butter. (This recipe makes more pesto than required for the soup. Refrigerate leftovers in a sealed container.)

To serve, ladle the soup into 4 warm bowls. Spoon a teaspoon of pesto onto the soup and swirl with the point of a knife. *Serves 4*

Rosemary Potato Skewers

Dress chunks of firm potatoes such as reds, Yellow Finns or White Rose with olive oil, rosemary and garlic. If grilling isn't in the plan, finish off these skewers in the broiler.

4 medium potatoes (approximately 1 1/3 pounds), peeled and cut into 1 1/2-inch chunks
1 tablespoon olive oil
1 tablespoon salted butter or margarine, melted
1 tablespoon chopped fresh rosemary or 1 teaspoon dried

1 large clove garlic, minced
1/2 teaspoon salt
1/4 teaspoon freshly ground black pepper

Four 12-inch metal skewers or 4 bamboo skewers soaked in warm water for 30 minutes

Prepare a charcoal grill or preheat the broiler.

In a heavy saucepan with a tight-fitting lid, cook the potatoes in 2 inches of salted boiling water until tender, approximately 15 minutes. Drain the potatoes, cool slightly and thread them onto metal or bamboo skewers.

In a small bowl, mix together the remaining ingredients. Place potato skewers on the grill 3 to 4 inches above the glowing embers. Brush the skewers with the rosemary mixture. Grill, basting and turning several times, until the potatoes are lightly browned, approximately 10 to 12 minutes. *Serves 4*

Left to right: Parmesan Potato Puffs and Hot Wheels

Parmesan Potato Puffs

For best results, use starchy russets or creamy Yukon Golds for the mashed potatoes in these puffy potato balls with crispy Parmesan-walnut jackets.

1/4 cup milk
3 cups unseasoned mashed potatoes
    (approximately 1 1/2 pounds potatoes)
1 egg, beaten
1 teaspoon salt
1 teaspoon baking powder
1/8 teaspoon freshly ground black pepper
1/4 cup finely chopped onion
2 tablespoons chopped fresh parsley
1 1/4 cups freshly grated Parmesan cheese
1 cup chopped walnuts
1/2 cup melted salted butter or margarine
Paprika, for dusting

In a large bowl, combine the milk, mashed potatoes, egg, salt, baking powder, pepper, onion, parsley and 1/4 cup of the cheese and mix thoroughly. Form the mixture into 15 balls.

On a large plate, mix the remaining cheese with the walnuts. Dip each ball into the melted butter, then roll in the Parmesan-walnut mixture to coat. Cover and refrigerate 2 to 24 hours.

To prepare for serving, preheat the oven to 325 degrees F. Place potato balls on an oiled baking sheet, spaced 1/8-inch apart. Bake in the oven for 35 to 45 minutes, until potatoes are puffed and lightly browned. Dust with paprika. *Serves 5 to 7*

Hot Wheels

Waxy White Rose or red potatoes make tender discs that roll right along with predinner drinks.

2 medium potatoes (approximately 2/3 pound)
1 tablespoon salted butter or margarine, melted

Hot Topping:
1 teaspoon chopped fresh rosemary or
    1/4 teaspoon dried
1/4 teaspoon lemon peel
Salt to taste

Hotter Topping:
1/8 teaspoon freshly ground black pepper
1/8 teaspoon cayenne pepper
Salt to taste

Hottest Topping:
1/8 teaspoon red pepper flakes
1 teaspoon chopped fresh basil or 1/4 teaspoon dried
Salt to taste

Preheat the oven to 450 degrees F.

Slice the potatoes into 1/4-inch rounds. Line the bottom of a greased 9-inch pie plate with a layer of potatoes, overlapping the slices slightly. Drizzle the melted butter on top.

In a small bowl, combine the ingredients for the desired topping. Sprinkle evenly over the potatoes. Cover and bake in the oven for 15 minutes. Uncover and bake for 10 minutes. Serve immediately.

To prepare in the microwave, follow the procedures above using a microwavable dish. Cover the dish with plastic wrap. Microwave for 5 minutes on full power. Uncover and microwave for 2 minutes. *Serves 2*

Potato Hummus with Pita Chips

*Hummus is traditionally made with garbanzo beans, but it can also be made with potatoes.
You might try Yukon Golds or Yellow Finns in this Middle Eastern-spiced dip.*

1 pound potatoes (3 medium), peeled and
    cut into 1-inch cubes
3 large cloves garlic
1/4 cup roasted sesame tahini (available in
    natural food and Middle Eastern stores)
1/4 cup fresh lemon juice
2 tablespoons olive oil
Approximately 2/3 cup water

1/2 teaspoon ground cumin
1/4 teaspoon cayenne pepper
1 to 1 1/2 teaspoons salt

Pita Chips:
3 to 4 seven-inch rounds of pita bread
Olive oil or melted butter

Red, green and yellow bell pepper strips

In a heavy saucepan with a tight-fitting lid, cook the potatoes and garlic in 2 inches of salted boiling water until tender, approximately 15 minutes.

Drain thoroughly and pass through a ricer or food mill into a bowl. Add the tahini, lemon juice and oil and blend thoroughly. Gradually stir in the water until the mixture is the proper consistency for dipping. Add the cumin and cayenne, then season with salt.

Preheat the oven to 350 degrees F.

Prepare the pita chips: Cut each pita bread into 8 triangles. Split open each triangle to make 2 triangles. Brush the surface of the triangles lightly with melted butter or olive oil. Place on a baking sheet. Bake for 5 to 10 minutes until chips are browned and crisp.

Serve the hummus at room temperature with tricolored pepper strips and pita chips.
Serves 6

Mixed Potato Antipasto

*Try this antipasto with a difference. A variety of potatoes are infused with
the flavors of lemon and cumin and served on a bed of bitter greens.*

*2 cups chicken stock, homemade or
    low-sodium canned*
Juice and grated zest of 1 lemon
1 teaspoon ground cumin
2 bay leaves
*1 pound potatoes (combination of white, Yukon
    Gold and/or Peruvian Blue potatoes),
    cut into 3/4-inch cubes*

*4 cups mixed bitter greens (such as watercress,
    purple and white kale), washed and dried*
6 ounces sliced salami
2/3 cup dry-cured black olives
*2/3 cup drained sun-dried tomatoes marinated in
    olive oil (reserve 3 tablespoons marinating oil)*
3 tablespoons chopped fresh parsley
1 tablespoon red wine vinegar
Salt and freshly ground black pepper to taste

In a 2- to 3-quart saucepan, combine the chicken stock, lemon juice and zest, cumin and bay leaves and bring to boil. Add the potatoes, reduce the heat, cover and simmer for approximately 15 minutes, until potatoes are just tender. Remove from the heat and let potatoes cool in the stock. Drain and set aside.

To serve, place the greens on a large platter. Arrange the potatoes, salami, olives and tomatoes over the greens. Sprinkle the arrangement with parsley. Drizzle the potatoes with the reserved marinating oil and the vinegar. Season with salt and pepper. *Serves 8 as an appetizer or 4 as a main course*

Crispy Dutch New Potatoes

*A small amount of sugar makes just the right glaze on these little reds,
seasoned with thyme and browned crumbs. By steaming the potatoes in shallow water,
rather than boiling them, their valuable nutrients don't leech out into the water.*

12 small red potatoes (approximately 2 pounds)
2 teaspoons sugar
2 tablespoons salted butter or margarine
1 1/2 teaspoons chopped fresh thyme or
   1/2 teaspoon dried

1 teaspoon salt
Freshly ground (preferably coarse grind)
   black pepper to taste
3/4 cup bread crumbs
Fresh parsley sprigs

In a heavy saucepan with a tight-fitting lid, cook the unpeeled potatoes in approximately 2 inches of salted water until almost tender, approximately 20 to 25 minutes. Drain and set aside.

Sprinkle the sugar into a hot, heavy skillet. When the sugar has melted, add the potatoes. Shake the potatoes in the pan continually and cook over medium-high heat, lightly browning the potatoes on all sides. Add the butter and continue to move the pan back and forth. Sprinkle the thyme, salt, pepper and bread crumbs over the potatoes. Shake the pan to distribute the bread crumbs evenly. Transfer to a serving dish. Garnish with parsley.

Serves 6 to 8

Pasilla Chilies Stuffed with Potatoes and Cheese

*Because of their firm texture, little cubes of White Rose potatoes would be as good
as the red potatoes in these Mexican-inspired stuffed chilies.*

*4 large fresh pasilla chilies (available at Mexican
    markets and specialty stores)*
1 tablespoon olive oil
*1 pound red potatoes (3 medium),
    cut into 1/3-inch cubes*
2 large cloves garlic, minced
*1 (2 1/2-inch long) jalapeño chili,
    seeds removed and minced*
2 tablespoons chopped fresh cilantro
1/2 teaspoon salt
1/8 teaspoon freshly ground black pepper

1 cup (4 ounces) shredded Monterey Jack cheese
1/4 cup freshly grated Parmesan cheese

Tomato Salsa:
2 medium tomatoes
1 small onion
12 sprigs cilantro
4 to 6 fresh serrano chilies
1 teaspoon sugar
2/3 cup fresh lime or orange juice, or water
Salt and freshly ground black pepper to taste

Slit the pasilla chilies lengthwise, leaving the stem ends intact. With the tip of a sharp paring knife, remove the seeds and membranes. Parboil the chilies in a pot of boiling water until just tender but not soft, approximately 6 to 8 minutes. Drain thoroughly and set aside in a shallow baking dish.

Preheat the oven to 400 degrees F. Heat the oil in a large skillet over medium-high heat. Add the potatoes, cover and cook for approximately 10 minutes, or until almost tender.

Uncover the potatoes and add the garlic. Cook over high heat until potatoes are brown, tossing occasionally. Add the jalapeño, cilantro, salt, pepper and cheeses and mix thoroughly. Using a spoon, stuff the pasilla chilies with the potato mixture. Cover with foil and bake until they are hot through and the cheese is melted.

While the pasilla chilies are baking, prepare the salsa: Chop the tomatoes, onion, cilantro and chilies coarsely and mix together in a medium bowl. Stir in the sugar and juice. Season to taste. Serve the salsa alongside the hot stuffed peppers. *Serves 4*

Pumpkin-Potato Ravioli with Lemon-Chive Butter

*Prepared pasta sheets help to create this New-Age ravioli with
a potato-pumpkin filling and a simple butter sauce.*

Roasted Garlic:
2 heads garlic
1 tablespoon olive oil
1/4 cup white wine

1 pound red potatoes (10 small),
*   cut into 1/2-inch cubes*
1 cup canned pumpkin purée
1/3 cup half-and-half
8 tablespoons salted butter
1 1/2 to 2 teaspoons chili powder
Salt and freshly ground black pepper to taste

Lemon-Chive Butter:
2 tablespoons salted butter
Grated zest of 2 lemons
Juice of 1 lemon
1/2 cup chopped fresh chives

24 four-inch square fresh pasta sheets or wonton
*   wrappers, cooked al dente and kept hot*
Whole chives and thin lemon slices, for garnish

To roast the garlic: Preheat the oven to 425 degrees F. Cut off the tops of the garlic heads to expose cloves. Rub surface with olive oil. Place the garlic heads in a small, ovenproof pan, add wine, and cover with aluminum foil. Bake until garlic is soft, approximately 1 hour. (This recipe will yield more garlic than required. Refrigerate leftovers wrapped in foil.)

In a heavy saucepan with a tight-fitting lid, cook potatoes in 2 inches of salted boiling water until tender, approximately 10 to 15 minutes. Drain and return the potatoes to the saucepan.

Mash the potatoes and add the pumpkin purée, half-and-half, butter, 1 teaspoon roasted garlic and the chili powder to the saucepan. Blend the mixture well. Season with salt and pepper. Set aside and keep hot.

Prepare the lemon-chive butter sauce: Melt the butter in a small saucepan. Stir in the lemon zest and juice and chopped chives. Set aside and keep warm over a low flame.

To serve, place 1 drained, cooked pasta sheet on each plate and spoon 1/4 cup of the potato-pumpkin mixture on top. Cover with another pasta sheet. Drizzle the ravioli with the butter sauce. Garnish with whole chives and lemon slices. *Serves 12 as an appetizer or 4 as a main dish*

Salad of Herbs with Potato Croutons

*In this unusual salad, golden brown potato croutons contrast nicely
with pungent herb flavors and a lemony dressing.*

Lemon Dressing:
1/4 cup olive oil
2 tablespoons champagne or white wine vinegar
1 tablespoon fresh lemon juice
2 tablespoons minced shallots
1/2 teaspoon salt
1/4 teaspoon freshly ground black pepper
1/2 to 1 teaspoon sugar, or to taste

Vegetable oil, for frying
*2/3 pound russet potatoes (2 medium), cut into
1/2-inch cubes and blotted on paper towels*
Lemon pepper
*10 cups loosely packed, cold herb sprigs and leaves
(choose a selection from watercress, arugula,
cilantro, mint, oregano, Italian parsley, basil
and dill), washed and dried*

Prepare the lemon dressing: In a small bowl, whisk together the olive oil, vinegar, lemon juice, shallots, salt and pepper. Whisk in enough sugar to balance the flavors. Set aside.

In an 8-inch skillet, heat 1/2 inch of vegetable oil to 375 degrees F. Fry potato cubes until nicely browned and cooked through, approximately 3 to 5 minutes. The oil should be hot, but not smoking and should bubble immediately around the potatoes. Remove the potatoes with a slotted spoon, drain on paper towels and sprinkle with lemon pepper.

In a large bowl, toss the herbs with dressing. Divide the herbs equally among 4 chilled plates. Top with the potato croutons.
Serves 4

ACCOMPANIMENTS

"With potatoes on the side" is a refrain sung in most restaurants and fast-food take-outs. This generally means fresh, hot fries, but there seems to be no end to the stylish and innovative ways to deal with the versatile spud in home kitchens and in better restaurants. If you're lucky, you can find roasted balsamic potatoes and onions, potato croquettes with a heavenly, tart tomato jam, Tuscan potato pancakes and the Irish national dish of Colcannon on the menu. If not, you can make them yourself.

In spite of all the innovations, the old-time classics are still my favorites. What's a steak without a perfectly baked potato? Did you know that the best mashed potatoes are baked first? Or that the best hashed browns are made with leftover baked potatoes and that the best scalloped potatoes are made with half-and-half and finished off with heavy cream? In this chapter, I've included my versions of the best potato accompaniments. Your way of making the best is probably just as good as mine.

The Best Scalloped Potatoes

Nobody knows how to make scalloped potatoes like the French.
Their potatoes never curdle, never separate, never taste like cheese and never have to be cut with a knife
when baked. The truth is, they don't call them scalloped at all—they call them gratin.
This is the way the potato expert Lydie Marshall does one version.

2 tablespoons salted butter, cold
2 pounds russet or Yukon Gold potatoes
 (6 medium), peeled and thinly sliced

1 1/2 teaspoons salt
1 l/2 cups half-and-half
1/2 cup heavy cream

Preheat the oven to 325 degrees F.

Rub 1 tablespoon of the butter on the bottom of a 2-quart baking dish. Overlap the potatoes in 3 layers, sprinkling each layer with a little salt. Pour the half-and-half over the potatoes, just enough to cover them, and dot the top with the remaining butter.

Bake in the middle of the oven for 45 minutes.

Spoon the heavy cream carefully over the top layer of potatoes and continue baking for another 45 minutes, or until golden brown.
Serves 6

The Best Skinny Fries

*So brown and crisp, you wouldn't believe these fries were never immersed in
a kettle of oil. Use russets, round whites or Yellow Finns.*

*4 medium potatoes (approximately 1 1/3 pounds),
uniform in size*
2 tablespoons vegetable oil
Salt to taste
Paprika to taste

Mustard Dill Dip:
1/4 cup unflavored yogurt
2 teaspoons thinly sliced green onions
1 1/2 teaspoons prepared mustard
1/4 teaspoon dried dill weed

1/8 teaspoon sugar
Salt and freshly ground black pepper to taste

Tomato Garden Dip:
1/4 cup finely chopped tomato
2 tablespoons finely chopped green pepper
1 tablespoon sliced green onion
1 tablespoon finely chopped parsley
1 1/2 teaspoons red wine vinegar
1 small clove garlic, minced

Preheat the oven to 450 degrees F.

Cut the potatoes into 1/2-inch sticks and place in a bowl of ice water to crisp. Drain and pat dry on paper towels. Arrange sticks in a single layer on a baking sheet. Sprinkle with oil. Shake pan to coat potatoes with oil. Bake in the oven until golden brown and tender, for 30 to 40 minutes, turning frequently. Sprinkle with salt and paprika.

Meanwhile, in separate small bowls, combine the dip ingredients and chill. Serve fries plain or with your choice of dips. *Serves 4*

The Best Baked Potatoes

*I consider the baked potato to be
the most healing and comforting of foods.
I'm picky about its shape and size.
It must have a well-netted, earthy skin which
tells me that this boy was grown and
harvested at the right time and place. It must be
a russet, approximately 12 ounces more or
less, because it will be my whole, well-balanced
meal. If you are making potatoes as part of
a meal, then shop for the ones that are
approximately 8 ounces, but bake them for
the same length of time.*

1 russet potato
2 tablespoons salted butter
Salt and freshly ground black pepper to taste

Preheat the oven to 400 degrees F.

Scrub the potato well. Put it into the middle rack of your oven and bake for an hour or more, until it is tender when pierced with a fork. Immediately slash the potato horizontally and vertically, pinch with your fingers into a snowy mound and top with butter, a little salt and pepper. *Serves 1*

A Happy Accident:
For the best hash browns, simply leave 2 baked potatoes in a turned-off oven overnight. The next day, peel, dice and sauté them in a little oil until brown and crisp. Sprinkle with salt and freshly ground black pepper. *Serves 2*

The Best Mashed Potatoes

*I think the best mashed potatoes
are baked first. Here they are. Earthy, light
as a cloud, the most potatoey flavor and
you don't have to peel them!*

2 pounds russet potatoes (6 medium)
1/4 cup heavy cream or crème fraîche
1/4 cup milk
8 tablespoons salted butter, cut into pieces
Salt and freshly ground black pepper to taste

Preheat the oven to 400 degrees F.

Wash the potatoes. Bake them in the oven for 1 hour, or until the flesh is very, very soft when pierced with a fork.

In a small saucepan, heat the cream and milk over low heat. Slash open the potatoes and scoop the flesh into a ricer or pass it through a coarse sieve into a warm bowl. With a fork, whip in the cream and milk mixture, the butter and season with salt and pepper. Mix in a little more milk for the correct consistency. Serve right away or keep warm over a pan of hot water, covered with plastic wrap, for up to 20 minutes. *Serves 6*

Note: For garlic mashed potatoes, mix in 4 to 6 cloves mashed roasted garlic (see p. 34) with the cream, butter, salt and pepper mixture.

Couch Potatoes

These unusual stuffed potatoes make good companions with poultry or pork.
Use high- or medium-starch potatoes such as russets, round whites or Yukon Golds.

4 medium potatoes (approximately 1 1/3 pounds),
  uniform in size
6 slices bacon
1/4 cup cider vinegar
1/4 cup milk

Salt and freshly ground black pepper to taste
1/2 cup sliced green onions
1 teaspoon poppy seeds
Chopped fresh parsley
Apple sauce and sour cream (optional)

Preheat the oven to 400 degrees F.

Wash the potatoes and pierce the skins with a fork. Bake in the oven until fork-tender, approximately 45 minutes. Let cool.

Meanwhile, cut the bacon into 1/2-inch pieces and cook in a broad skillet over high heat until crisp. Drain bacon on paper towels. Reserve 1 tablespoon of bacon drippings in the skillet.

Slice off the top third of the potatoes, horizontally. With a melon baller, scoop out the pulp, reserving the skins. Heat bacon drippings and add potato pulp and vinegar. Cook over medium heat until potatoes absorb all the liquid. Remove from the heat.

With a potato masher, mash potatoes with milk and season with salt and pepper. Mix in the bacon, green onions and poppy seeds. Spoon the mixture into the potato skins. Bake in the oven 10 minutes until heated through. Garnish with chopped parsley. Serve with applesauce and sour cream on the side, if desired. *Serves 4*

Note: Couch potatoes may be prepared ahead and refrigerated. To serve, cover loosely with foil, and bake at 375 degrees F. for approximately 20 minutes, or until heated through.

Colcannon

*This potato and cabbage dish is the perfect partner for corned beef. Make the mashed potatoes
for this Irish mainstay with mealy russets or creamier, yellow Yukon Golds.*

1 red or green cabbage (approximately 3 pounds)
2 tablespoons salted butter or margarine
3 cups hot unseasoned mashed potatoes
    (approximately 1 1/2 pounds potatoes)
1/4 cup milk

1/3 cup sliced green onions
1 teaspoon salt
1/2 teaspoon nutmeg
Chopped fresh parsley

Remove core from cabbage. Carefully hollow out cabbage from core end, leaving a shell approximately 1 inch thick. Set aside the cabbage.

    Place cabbage shell in a Dutch oven and cover with boiling water (shell will float). Cover and cook over medium-high heat for 10 to 15 minutes, or until crisp-tender. Drain and set aside.

Meanwhile, coarsely chop the reserved cabbage. In a large skillet, melt butter over medium heat. Add the chopped cabbage and cook until crisp yet tender. Stir in the potatoes and milk. Add the green onions, salt and nutmeg. Mix to blend thoroughly and heat through.

    Carefully place the cabbage shell on a serving plate, with the hollow side facing up. Spoon the potato mixture into the shell. Sprinkle with parsley. Cut into wedges and serve hot.

Serves 6

Natural Hash Browns with their Skins

Most dishes can use potatoes au naturel—with their skins. It certainly makes
life easier when you don't have to peel the spuds. These hash browns
are good with just about anything, and just about every potato variety works well,
although the starchier ones will have a softer texture.

2/3 pound potatoes (2 medium), unpeeled
1 1/2 teaspoons salted butter or margarine
1 1/2 teaspoons vegetable oil
1/2 cup chopped onion

1/2 teaspoon dried herbs of your choice
  (such as thyme or tarragon)
2 tablespoons chopped fresh parsley
Salt and freshly ground black pepper to taste

Coarsely grate potatoes into a strainer or colander. Rinse under cold running water and pat dry between paper toweling.

In a broad nonstick skillet, heat butter and oil. Add the potatoes, onion and herbs and cook over medium-high heat until potatoes are tender and golden, tossing occasionally to brown evenly. Add parsley. Season with salt and pepper. Serve hot. *Serves 2*

Crisp Potato Skins

Crunchy skins are almost addictive. They're great
with burgers and make tasty snacks all by themselves.

4 medium potatoes (1 1/3 pounds), such as
russets, round whites or Yukon Gold,
uniform in size
2 tablespoons safflower oil

Dash of hot pepper sauce
1 teaspoon low-sodium soy sauce
1/4 teaspoon minced garlic

Preheat the oven to 400 degrees F.

Wash the potatoes and pierce skins with the tines of a fork. Bake in the oven until fork-tender, approximately 45 minutes. Slightly cool the potatoes; quarter lengthwise, then halve crosswise to make 8 sections. Scoop the pulp from the skins, leaving shells 1/8 inch thick.

(Reserve pulp for use in other recipes calling for mashed potatoes.)

Raise the oven heat to 500 degrees F. In a small bowl, mix the safflower oil with hot pepper sauce, soy sauce and/or minced garlic. Place skins on a baking sheet and brush on both sides with oil mixture. Bake until crisp, approximately 12 to 15 minutes. *Serves 4*

Warm Potato Salad

Peruvian Blues would be a good option here, as well as
round whites or Yukon Golds—all these potatoes will easily absorb the brothy marinade.
Baked chicken or grilled vegetables go deliciously with this dish.

1 1/3 pounds potatoes (4 medium),
    sliced 1/4 inch thick
1 1/3 cups chicken stock, homemade or
    low-sodium canned
1/3 cup vegetable oil

2 tablespoons white wine vinegar
2 teaspoons grainy mustard
Salt and freshly ground black pepper to taste
Chopped fresh parsley

In a large saucepan, combine the potatoes and stock. Bring to a boil, reduce heat, cover and simmer until just tender, approximately 10 minutes. Remove from the heat; drain and reserve stock from the potatoes.

Combine 1/4 cup of the stock (reserving remaining stock for another use), the oil, vinegar, mustard, salt and pepper. Whisk to blend. Pour over potatoes, tossing gently to coat. Let stand for 10 minutes to serve warm, or serve at room temperature. Garnish with parsley. *Serves 4*

Potato Croquettes with Tomato Jam

Cinnamon-spiced fresh tomato jam, an old-fashioned specialty, makes a tasty mate for crispy potato croquettes. Try this combination with roast or baked chicken.

Tomato Jam:
1 pound tomatoes, cut into 3/4-inch chunks (approximately 2 1/2 cups)
3/4 cup sugar
Juice of 1 lemon
2 teaspoons grated fresh ginger
1/2 teaspoon cinnamon

1 1/2 pounds russet potatoes (4 to 5 medium), peeled and cut into 1 1/2-inch chunks
1/3 cup sliced green onions
3 tablespoons chopped fresh parsley
1 egg, beaten
1 teaspoon salt
1/4 teaspoon freshly ground black pepper
Vegetable oil
1 cup yellow corn meal

Prepare the tomato jam: In a 2- to 3-quart saucepan, combine all the ingredients. Bring to a boil, reduce heat, cover and simmer approximately 45 minutes, stirring occasionally, until the consistency of thin jam. Let cool. Refrigerate in a covered container.

In a saucepan with a tight-fitting lid, cook potatoes in 2 inches of salted boiling water until tender, approximately 20 minutes. Drain and pass through a ricer into a large bowl. Add onions, parsley, egg, salt and pepper. Mix to blend thoroughly. Form into 8 patties 1/2 inch thick.

Meanwhile, in a large skillet, heat approximately 1/2 inch oil to 375 degrees F. The oil should be hot, but not smoking and should bubble immediately around the patties. Roll potato patties in cornmeal to coat, then fry until browned on both sides, approximately 6 minutes, turning once. Remove with slotted spatula and drain on paper towels. Repeat until all the croquettes are fried. Serve hot with tomato jam on the side. *Serves 4*

Tuscan Baked Potato Pancakes

When you're baking russets for dinner, bake enough to make these plump potato pancakes the next day. A crispy cornmeal coating encases a moist, flavorful interior. Try these with grilled steak or chops.

*1 pound of leftover baked potato pulp
  (approximately 2 cups)
1/2 cup shredded sharp Cheddar cheese
1/4 cup chopped, prepared roasted red bell peppers
2 green onions, sliced
1 egg, beaten
1 tablespoon chopped fresh basil, 1 1/2 teaspoons
  chopped fresh oregano, 1 teaspoon chopped
  fresh rosemary and 1 teaspoon chopped fresh
  thyme, or 2 teaspoons dried Italian herbs
Dash of hot pepper sauce
Salt and freshly ground black pepper to taste
Cornmeal, for coating pancakes
Vegetable oil, for sautéing*

In a large bowl, combine all ingredients except salt, pepper, cornmeal and oil. Season with salt and pepper to taste.

Form the potato mixture into four 1/2-inch thick pancakes and coat with cornmeal. Sauté in oil over high heat until the pancakes are crisp and golden brown, turning once. Serve hot. *Serves 4*

Roasted Balsamic Potatoes and Onions

*In this dish, potatoes and onions, a favorite combination, are handsomely
glazed with heady balsamic vinegar. The flavors stand up to roasted meats and steak.
In addition to reds, Yellow Finns would work fine, too.*

2 tablespoons olive oil
*1 1/4 to 1 1/2 pounds red potatoes, halved
    (larger red potatoes cut into 1-inch chunks)*
*3/4 pound onions, peeled, leaving root ends
    intact, cut into 3/4-inch wedges*

1/4 cup balsamic vinegar
*1 tablespoon fresh thyme or
    1 teaspoon dried*
1/2 teaspoon salt, or to taste
1/4 teaspoon freshly ground black pepper

Preheat the oven to 400 degrees F.

Pour oil into a 10 1/2- x 15 1/2-inch (jellyroll) pan. Add the potatoes and onions and toss to coat with oil. Cover with foil and roast for 30 minutes. Remove the foil.

Increase the heat to 450 degrees F. Add remaining ingredients and toss thoroughly. Continue to roast, tossing occasionally, for 30 to 40 minutes, or until vegetables are browned and potatoes are crisp on the edges. *Serves 4*

MAIN COURSES

You can't go wrong with potatoes, I always say. For the main event you can play it safe with a big goulash soup, crusty bread and crispy greens. A rich chicken soup bubbling in the pot with feather-light potato dumplings never fails to please. One of the more unusual ways to whet the appetite is with brandade, the wonderfully flavorful dish of salt cod mellowed with potatoes and garlic served in the south of France. Roast potato pie with salmon fillets and Gruyère is a good fix-and-forget casserole that never ceases to comfort, as do most of the potato dishes in this section.

There are many tricks with potatoes to help you gussy up a piece of fish or a simple roast chicken. Saffron mashed potatoes is one that I particularly love because the bright tomato-fennel sauce is just the right counterpart to the exotic yellow saffron. And there are always special-occasion dishes that titillate like the patriotic Fourth of July salad of red, white and blue potatoes.

Hearty Goulash Soup

*White Rose potatoes keep their identity when cooked in this old-country,
stick-to-the-ribs soup filled with vegetables and tender chunks of beef.*

4 slices bacon, cut into 1-inch strips
2 cups sliced onions
2 tablespoons paprika
1 tablespoon salt
1/2 teaspoon freshly ground black pepper
1/2 teaspoon caraway seeds (optional)
1 bay leaf
2 cloves garlic, minced

2 pounds beef chuck, trimmed and
    cut into 1- to 1 1/2-inch cubes
1 can (14 1/2 ounces) stewed tomatoes
3 cups water
1 small green bell pepper, cut into 1-inch pieces
1 1/2 cups sliced mushrooms
1 1/3 pounds potatoes (4 medium), cut into
    1-inch cubes
Sour cream and chopped green onions, for garnish

In a Dutch oven, cook the bacon over medium heat until crisp; remove with slotted spoon and set aside. Drain all but 3 tablespoons of fat. Add the onions to the Dutch oven and sauté for 5 minutes. Stir in the paprika, salt, pepper, caraway seeds, bay leaf and garlic. Add the beef, tomatoes and 2 cups of the water and stir together. Bring to a boil, reduce the heat, cover, and simmer for 1 to 1 1/2 hours, or until beef is tender.

Add cooked bacon, remaining water, green pepper, mushrooms and potatoes. Bring to a boil, reduce heat and simmer until potatoes are tender, approximately 20 minutes.

To serve, ladle soup into individual bowls. Add a dollop of sour cream to each and sprinkle with green onions, if desired. *Serves 6 to 8*

Potato, Leek and Gorgonzola Phyllo Pie

Sturdy reds, Yukon Golds or White Rose potatoes would be excellent in this crackly crusted pie.

7 tablespoons salted butter
3 1/2 cups sliced leeks (approximately 6 leeks),
*   white part only*
2 shallots, minced
1/2 pound potatoes (2 medium), thinly sliced

Salt and freshly ground black pepper to taste
6 sheets (14- x 18-inch) phyllo dough
1/2 cup chopped toasted walnuts
2/3 cup crumbled Gorgonzola cheese
1/4 cup half-and-half

Melt 2 tablespoons of butter in a 12-inch nonstick skillet over medium heat. Add the leeks and shallots and cook, stirring occasionally, for approximately 5 minutes, or until softened. Remove from the skillet and reserve.

In the same skillet, melt 2 more tablespoons of butter over medium heat. Add the potato slices. Cook for approximately 5 minutes on each side, until the potatoes are crisp. Season with salt and pepper and set aside.

Preheat the oven to 425 degrees F. To make the pie, in a small saucepan, melt the remaining 3 tablespoons of butter. Lay 2 phyllo sheets in a single layer on a clean work surface and brush with a little melted butter. Place the sheets in a 9-inch pie plate, allowing sheets to extend over edge. Repeat the process with the remaining phyllo and melted butter. Layer half of the leeks, potatoes, walnuts and cheese. Repeat. Pour the half-and-half on top.

Gather the phyllo dough up over the center of pie to cover top. Brush with the remaining melted butter. Bake the pie for approximately 20 minutes, or until phyllo is crisp and golden brown. Let stand for 5 minutes before cutting into wedges. *Serves 6*

Roast Potato Pie

Select Yukon Gold or White Rose potatoes for this layered casserole that includes fresh salmon fillets and Gruyère cheese. It's an elegant supper dish to pair with a simple salad of Belgian endive.

2 pounds potatoes (6 medium)
Juice of 1/2 lemon
1/4 cup unsalted butter
1 medium onion, grated and drained
4 large cloves garlic, minced
1/2 teaspoon salt

1/2 teaspoon freshly ground black pepper
3/4 pound salmon fillets, skinned and
*   cut diagonally into 1/4-inch long slices*
2 cups shredded Gruyère cheese
1/4 cup freshly grated aged Romano or
*   Parmesan cheese*

Peel the potatoes and place in a large bowl of ice water mixed with lemon juice. With a mandoline or sharp knife, slice the potatoes very thin (the thickness of potato chips). Return the slices to the bowl of ice water.

Melt 3 tablespoons of the butter in a medium-sized skillet over medium heat. Add the onion, garlic, salt and pepper and sauté until onion is transparent. Remove from the heat and set aside.

Preheat the oven to 375 degrees F. Grease a deep 9- or 10-inch pie dish or casserole with 1 tablespoon of the remaining butter. Make a layer of drained potato slices on the bottom of the dish. Top with a layer of the onion mixture, salmon slices and cheeses, using 4 layers of each and ending with 2 layers of potato slices on top. Brush with the remaining tablespoon of butter, melted.

Cover with aluminum foil and bake in the oven for 30 minutes. Remove the foil and continue to bake until potatoes are tender throughout, approximately 15 minutes. Remove from the oven and set aside for 10 minutes. Cut into wedges with a sharp knife.
Serves 6

Bacon and Potato Stuffing for Savory Birds

Made with the pulp from baked russet potatoes, this smoky-flavored potato stuffing studded with bread cubes and bits of bacon is an ideal accompaniment for chicken, turkey or game hens.

2 1/2 pounds potatoes (7 to 8 medium), baked
1/2 pound bacon, cut into 1/2-inch pieces
1 1/2 cups coarsely chopped onion
1 cup sliced celery
1 tablespoon chopped fresh sage
1 1/2 teaspoons chopped fresh thyme

3/4 cup water
1/4 cup salted butter or margarine, melted
1 cup seasoned bread crumbs, homemade or
    prepared
1/4 cup chopped fresh parsley
Salt and freshly ground black pepper to taste

Scoop the pulp from baked potatoes, break up and measure approximately 1 quart. Set aside. (Save potato skins for another occasion.★)

In a large skillet, cook the bacon until crisp. Drain all but 2 tablespoons of fat. Add the onion and celery to the skillet and cook for 2 minutes. Add the potato pulp, sage and thyme and mix well.

In a large bowl, pour water and butter over bread cubes; toss to moisten evenly. Mix in the potato mixture and parsley. Season with salt and pepper. Use to stuff your holiday bird.

To make stuffing balls instead: Moisten with additional water as needed to shape into 3-inch balls. Place on a greased baking sheet. Drizzle with additional melted butter, if desired. Bake at 350 degrees F. for 25 to 30 minutes, until golden. *Makes approximately 12 cups stuffing, 14 to 16 stuffing balls with extra to be baked in a casserole, or enough for 1 large turkey*

★ *Note:* For crispy potato skins, brush skins with olive oil or butter, sprinkle with salt and pepper and bake in a hot oven until crisp.

Brandade with Potatoes

*Mealy russets or creamier Yukon Golds carry the flavors of salt cod, lemon juice
and garlic in this briny dish with origins in Provence.*

1 pound boneless and skinless salt cod
1 medium onion, halved
2 large cloves garlic, halved
1 bay leaf
3/4 pound russet potatoes (2 to 3 medium),
    peeled and cut into 1/4-inch chunks
3/4 cup milk

1/2 cup extra virgin olive oil
2 hard-boiled eggs
1 large clove garlic, minced
2 tablespoons chopped fresh parsley
1 tablespoon sherry wine vinegar
Salt, freshly ground black pepper and
    lemon juice to taste

Place the cod in a colander and set under running cold water for 5 minutes. Transfer to a bowl and cover with cold water. Set aside for approximately 8 hours, changing the water every couple of hours.

Rinse the cod thoroughly in cold water and cut into 4 or 5 pieces. Place in a large saucepan, cover with water and add the onion, garlic and bay leaf. Bring to a boil and simmer until cod is opaque and flakes easily, approximately 10 minutes.

With a slotted spoon, remove the cod from the liquid and transfer to the bowl of a food processor.

Add the potatoes to the liquid in the saucepan. Bring to a boil and cook until tender, approximately 15 minutes.

Meanwhile, in another small saucepan, heat the milk and 6 tablespoons of oil over low heat. Add half of the milk mixture into the food processor and pulse on and off until coarsely blended with the cod. Pour in the remaining milk mixture and pulse on and off until mixture is well blended but not smooth.

When the potatoes are tender, drain and heat over low heat until all the moisture evaporates. Remove and discard the bay leaf and onion. Pass the potatoes and eggs through a food mill into a large bowl.

Mix in the remaining 2 tablespoons oil and the minced garlic. Fold the cod mixture into the potato mixture. Mix in the parsley and vinegar. Season with salt, pepper and lemon juice. Serve at room temperature with garlic toasts. *Serves 4 as a main course or 12 as an appetizer*

Warm Blue Potatoes and White Beans
with Sautéed Shrimp

This colorful dish with bright lime and herbal flavors can be moved outdoors to the barbecue grill.
Simply toss the shrimp with dressing, thread onto skewers and grill over glowing coals.

1 pound (3 medium) Peruvian Blue potatoes,
  sliced 1/2 inch thick

Dressing:
1/2 cup olive oil
1/4 cup fresh lime juice
1/4 cup finely chopped red onion
1/4 cup chopped fresh mint
3 tablespoons chopped fresh cilantro
1 teaspoon salt
1/2 teaspoon sugar
1/4 teaspoon freshly ground black pepper

1 1/4 pounds medium shrimp, shelled and
  deveined
1/2 cup sun-dried tomatoes marinated in
  olive oil, drained
1 can (15 ounces) canellini or other white beans,
  rinsed and drained
Mint sprigs

In a heavy saucepan with a tight-fitting lid, cook the potatoes in 2 inches of salted boiling water until barely tender, approximately 10 to 15 minutes. Drain and set aside.

Prepare the dressing: In a small bowl, whisk the oil, lime juice, onion, mint, cilantro, salt, sugar and pepper. Spoon 1/4 cup dressing into a large skillet over medium-high heat. Add the shrimp and sauté until opaque throughout.

Meanwhile, pour the remaining dressing over the potatoes in the saucepan and add the tomatoes. Toss gently over low heat until warm. Add the beans and toss gently to heat through. Spoon onto 4 warm plates and divide the shrimp equally on top. Garnish with mint sprigs. *Serves 4*

Saffron Mashed Potatoes with Grilled Fish and Tomato-Fennel Sauce

*Yukon Gold or russet potatoes are best for mashing
or ricing, so they work well in this meal. The saffron potatoes would also be
delicious with roast lamb or grilled lamb chops.*

1 1/3 pounds potatoes, peeled and
    cut into 1 1/2-inch chunks

Tomato-Fennel Sauce:
2 tablespoons salted butter
3/4 cup thinly sliced fennel bulb
1/2 cup coarsely chopped onion
2 cups coarsely chopped tomatoes
2/3 cup dry white wine
Salt and freshly ground black pepper to taste

2/3 cup milk
3 tablespoons salted butter
1/4 teaspoon saffron filaments, crushed
Salt to taste
1/8 teaspoon white pepper
Four 6-ounce firm white fish fillets (such as
    monkfish, halibut or sea bass)

In a heavy saucepan with a tight-fitting lid, cook the potatoes in 2 inches of salted boiling water until tender, approximately 20 minutes.

Meanwhile, prepare the tomato-fennel sauce: Over medium heat, melt the butter in a 10-inch skillet. Add the fennel bulb and onion. Sauté approximately 5 minutes, or until onion is transparent. Add the tomatoes and wine. Simmer for approximately 10 minutes, until the mixture is reduced to a sauce consistency. Season with salt and pepper to taste. Keep hot.

Drain the potatoes and pass through a ricer or food mill into a large bowl. In a small saucepan, heat the milk, butter and saffron until the butter melts. Gradually add the milk mixture to the potatoes, beating with a whisk. Season with salt and pepper and keep warm in a double boiler or over hot water.

Meanwhile, prepare a charcoal grill or broiler. Season the fish with salt, and grill or broil for approximately 10 minutes per inch of thickness, turning once, until fish is opaque throughout. To serve, spoon sauce onto 4 plates and top with potatoes and fish. *Serves 4*

Salade Niçoise

This is another version of the classic tuna salad from France.
Tender Yukon Gold potatoes add a golden touch to the crisp-tender vegetables.

6 medium potatoes (approximately 2 pounds),
    sliced 1/4 inch thick
3/4 pound assorted fresh vegetables (asparagus,
    green beans, snow peas, broccoli florets),
    cooked until crisp-tender
2 medium tomatoes, sliced
1 cup sliced mushrooms
1 bunch radishes, trimmed
2 cans (6 1/2 or 6 3/4 ounces each) tuna,
    drained and flaked
Lettuce leaves, to line a platter
Parsley sprigs, for garnish

Niçoise Dressing:
3/4 cup vegetable oil
6 tablespoons white wine vinegar
3 tablespoons water
3 tablespoons chopped fresh parsley
1 1/2 tablespoons capers, drained
1 1/2 teaspoons dry mustard
1 large clove garlic, minced
1 1/2 teaspoons chopped fresh basil or
    1/2 teaspoon dried

In a 2-quart saucepan with a tight-fitting lid, cook the potatoes in 2 inches of salted boiling water just until tender, approximately 15 minutes. Drain and set aside.

Meanwhile, prepare the Niçoise dressing: In a small bowl, whisk together the oil, vinegar, water, parsley, capers, mustard, garlic and basil. Refrigerate to blend flavors. Whisk before serving. Toss the potatoes in a large bowl with half of the dressing. Cover and chill.

To serve, arrange the marinated potatoes, cooked vegetables, tomatoes, mushrooms, radishes and tuna on a lettuce-lined platter. Garnish with parsley. Pass the remaining dressing separately. *Serves 6*

Country French Potato Salad

Choose White Rose, any of the red or fingerling potatoes for this country garden salad.

1 1/3 pounds potatoes (4 medium),
    sliced 1/3 inch thick
2 cups fresh cooked peas or 1 package (10 ounces)
    frozen peas, thawed

Garden Mint Dressing:
1/4 cup vegetable oil
3 tablespoons cider vinegar
2 tablespoons water
1 teaspoon dry mustard
1 teaspoon honey
1/4 cup sliced green onions
3 tablespoons chopped fresh mint
Salt to taste

4 chicken breast halves, boned, skinned, poached,
    drained and cooled
Radishes and fresh mint sprigs, for garnish

In a heavy saucepan with a tight-fitting lid, cook potatoes in 2 inches of salted boiling water until tender, approximately 15 minutes. Drain and let cool.

Prepare the garden mint dressing: In a small bowl, whisk together the oil, vinegar, water, mustard and honey. Stir in the green onions, mint and salt to taste.

In a large bowl, toss potatoes and peas with half the dressing. In another bowl, toss the chicken with remaining dressing. Refrigerate.

To serve, arrange the potato mixture on a platter. Cut chicken into 1/3-inch slices and place on top. Drizzle with any remaining dressing. Garnish with radishes and mint. *Serves 4*

Red, White and Blue Potato Salad

This is one picnic salad that doesn't need to be limited to the Fourth of July or the backyard.

1 1/2 pounds assorted red, White Rose and
    Peruvian Blue potatoes (4 to 5 medium),
    cut into 3/4-inch cubes
5 tablespoons olive oil
3 tablespoons white wine vinegar
2 cloves garlic, minced
Salt and freshly cracked black pepper to taste
6 ounces smoked salmon, cut into 1-inch strips
1/3 cup roughly chopped chives
1/4 cup drained and rinsed capers
Whole chives and paprika

In a heavy saucepan with a tight-fitting lid, cook potatoes in 2 inches of salted boiling water until tender, approximately 15 to 20 minutes. Drain and set aside.

Meanwhile, in a large bowl, whisk together the oil, vinegar and garlic. Season with salt and pepper. Add potatoes, salmon, chopped chives and capers and toss gently. Garnish with whole chives and paprika. Serve warm or at room temperature. *Serves 4 to 6*

Left: Red, White and Blue Potato Salad
Right: Country French Potato Salad

Ranch Scramble

Here's a substantial dish for an authentic chuck wagon–style brunch.
Serve it at home on the range with fresh fruit on the side.

1 1/3 pounds russet potatoes (4 medium),
    uniform in size
1/4 cup salted butter
2 tablespoons olive oil
1 green bell pepper, cut into 1/2-inch chunks
4 green onions, sliced
1/2 pound deli roast beef, cut into
    1/2-inch chunks

1/2 cup prepared barbecue sauce
Salt and freshly ground black pepper to taste
8 eggs
1/4 cup milk
4 slices Texas toast (white bread sliced 1 inch
    thick, toasted on both sides)
Paprika, for garnish

Preheat the oven to 350 degrees F.

Pierce the potatoes with the tines of a fork. Bake in the oven for approximately 45 minutes, or until tender when pierced with a fork. Or to save time, bake in a microwave for 6 minutes.

Cut the potatoes into 3/4-inch cubes. Melt 2 tablespoons of the butter with the oil in a large skillet over medium-high heat and add the potatoes. Cook, tossing occasionally, for 5 minutes. Add the green pepper and onion and cook for an additional 5 minutes, tossing occasionally, until potatoes are crisp, golden brown and cooked through. Stir in the beef and barbecue sauce. Cook just to heat through. Season with salt and pepper. Cover and keep warm over a double boiler or over low heat.

In a small bowl, beat the eggs with the milk. In another large skillet, melt the remaining 2 tablespoons butter over medium-low heat. Add the egg mixture and gently stir until eggs are set and soft, but not dry. Season with salt and pepper.

To serve, place 1 slice of toast on each plate, top with some potato mixture and eggs. Sprinkle lightly with paprika. *Serves 4*

Mediterranean Fish and Potato Stew

Orange peel, fennel seeds and herbs add their magic to this tasty stew.
Round whites or any of the red potatoes would work well.

3 cans (14 1/2 ounces each) stewed tomatoes
1 clove garlic, minced
1 bay leaf
1 tablespoon chopped fresh basil or
    1 teaspoon dried
1 tablespoon chopped fresh thyme or
    1 teaspoon dried
1/2 teaspoon fennel seeds
Peel from 1/2 orange, cut in 1 continuous strip,
    1/4-inch wide

1/4 to 1/2 teaspoon red pepper flakes
1 pound potatoes (3 medium),
    sliced 1/4 inch thick
1/2 pound carrots (3 medium),
    sliced 1/8 inch thick
1 pound fresh halibut (or other firm white fish)
    fillets, cut into 2-inch chunks
2 cups fresh peas or 1 package (10 ounces)
    frozen peas, thawed
2 tablespoons freshly grated Parmesan cheese

In a Dutch oven, combine the tomatoes, garlic, bay leaf, basil, thyme, fennel seeds, orange peel, pepper flakes, potatoes and carrots. Cover and bring to a boil over medium heat. Reduce heat and simmer for approximately 20 minutes, stirring occasionally, until potatoes and carrots are tender.

Add the fish and peas and stir gently. Cover and simmer for an additional 5 to 10 minutes, until fish is opaque throughout. Remove the orange peel and bay leaf.

    Ladle into warm, shallow soup bowls and sprinkle with cheese. *Serves 4*

Cheer-Up Chicken Soup with Potato Dumplings

This chicken vegetable soup is very fast to make, and especially inviting when crowned with fluffy potato dumplings. Use any waxy potato for the soup and starchy russets for the dumplings.

Potato Dumplings:
1 cup unseasoned mashed potatoes
    (made from 1/2 pound potatoes)
1/4 cup flour
1/2 teaspoon salt
1/4 teaspoon pepper
1/4 teaspoon nutmeg
3 tablespoons sliced green onions
3 tablespoons chopped parsley
1 egg

3 2/3 cups chicken stock, homemade or
    low-sodium canned
2 cups water
3 chicken breast halves, skinned and boned
1/2 cup thinly sliced carrots
1/2 cup thinly sliced celery
1 medium potato, cut into 1/2-inch dice
1 1/2 cups sliced mushrooms
1/3 cup thinly sliced green onions
1 teaspoon chopped fresh thyme or
    1/4 teaspoon dried
Salt and freshly ground black pepper to taste

Prepare the potato dumpling dough: In a large bowl, mix together all the ingredients and set aside.

In a 3- to 4-quart saucepan, combine the stock and water and bring to boil. Meanwhile, cut chicken into 1/2-inch chunks and add to the liquid along with the carrots, celery and potato. Simmer for 10 minutes. Skim the scum off the top.

Meanwhile, in a Dutch oven, bring 3 quarts of salted water to a boil for the dumplings. Add the mushrooms, green onions and thyme to the soup. Simmer for an additional 10 minutes. Season with salt and pepper and keep hot. Divide the dumpling dough into 12 balls. Cook the dumplings in the boiling water for approximately 10 minutes.

Ladle the soup into large shallow soup bowls. Drain the dumplings with a slotted spoon and divide equally among the soup bowls. *Serves 4 to 6*

Winter Potato Stew

This stew is a one-dish meal that can be made a day or two ahead.
Any potato is delicious in this recipe, but the White Rose is an especially fitting choice
because it holds together well during the prolonged cooking.

1/3 cup all-purpose flour
1 teaspoon salt
1 teaspoon freshly ground black pepper
1 teaspoon paprika
2 pounds boneless lean beef, cut into 2-inch cubes
1/4 cup vegetable oil
1 large onion, peeled and sliced
4 celery stalks, sliced
4 cups water
1 bay leaf

1 tablespoon chopped fresh thyme or
*   1 teaspoon dried*
Salt and freshly ground black pepper to taste
2 pounds potatoes (6 medium), peeled and
*   cut into 3/4-inch cubes*
3 large carrots, cut into 1-inch pieces
1 small green bell pepper, cut into
*   3/4-inch chunks*
Chopped fresh parsley

Combine the flour, salt, pepper and paprika in a plastic bag. Add the beef cubes, a few pieces at a time, shaking to coat.

In a Dutch oven over medium-high heat, heat the oil. Add the beef and brown on all sides. Add the onion, celery and any excess flour mixture. Cook, stirring constantly for 2 minutes. Add the water, bay leaf, and thyme. Season with salt and pepper. Bring to a boil, cover, reduce heat and simmer until meat is tender, approximately 1 1/2 hours.

Stir in the potatoes and carrots. Replace the cover and cook for 20 minutes. Add the bell pepper and cook until vegetables are tender, approximately 5 to 10 minutes. Ladle into warm bowls. Sprinkle with parsley. *Serves 6*

INDEX

ACKNOWLEDGEMENTS

I'd like to thank Zelda Gordon, Diana Torrey and Beverly Yamanaka from the Ketchum Food Center; The Potato Board; Dr. John S. Niederhauser; and Geraldene Holt, *The Gourmet Garden*, Bulfinch Press, Little, Brown and Company. —Maggie Waldron

Collins and the photography team would also like to thank Jeri Jones and Helga Sigvaldadottir, photo assistants; Sara Slavin, props; Elise Calanchini, Inge Hoogerhuis and Vicki Roberts-Russell, food styling assistants; Cecile Chronister, design and production assistant; and Jonathan Mills and Lynne Noone, production managers. Special thanks to Mary Novak; Ron and Pam Kaiser; Cie Callaway; Westside Farms in Healdsburg, California; and Ronniger's Seed Potatoes.

Approximate Metric Conversions

Liquid Weights

U.S. Measurements	Metric Equivalents
1/4 teaspoon	1.23 ml
1/2 teaspoon	2.5 ml
3/4 teaspoon	3.7 ml
1 teaspoon	5 ml
1 dessertspoon	10 ml
1 tablespoon (3 teaspoons)	15 ml
2 tablespoons (1 ounce)	30 ml
1/4 cup	60 ml
1/3 cup	80 ml
1/2 cup	120 ml
2/3 cup	160 ml
3/4 cup	180 ml
1 cup (8 ounces)	240 ml
2 cups (1 pint)	480 ml
3 cups	720 ml
4 cups (1 quart)	1 litre
4 quarts (1 gallon)	3 3/4 litres

Dry Weights

U.S. Measurements	Metric Equivalents
1/4 ounce	7 grams
1/3 ounce	10 grams
1/2 ounce	14 grams
1 ounce	28 grams
1 1/2 ounces	42 grams
1 3/4 ounces	50 grams
2 ounces	57 grams
3 ounces	85 grams
3 1/2 ounces	100 grams
4 ounces (1/4 pound)	114 grams
6 ounces	170 grams
8 ounces (1/2 pound)	227 grams
9 ounces	250 grams
16 ounces (1 pound)	464 grams

Temperatures

Farenheit	Celsius (Centigrade)
32°F (water freezes)	0°C
200°F	95°C
212°F (water boils)	100°C
250°F	120°C
275°F	135°C
300°F (slow oven)	150°C
325°F	160°C
350°F (moderate oven)	175°C
375°F	190°C
400°F (hot oven)	205°C
425°F	220°C
450°F (very hot oven)	230°C
475°F	245°C
500°F (extremely hot oven)	260°C

Length

U.S. Measurements	Metric Equivalents
1/8 inch	3 mm
1/4 inch	6 mm
3/8 inch	1 cm
1/2 inch	1.2 cm
1 inch	2.5 cm
3/4 inch	2 cm
1 1/4 inches	3.1 cm
1 1/2 inches	3.7 cm
2 inches	5 cm
3 inches	7.5 cm
4 inches	10 cm
5 inches	12.5 cm

Approximate Equivalents

1 kilo is slightly more than 2 pounds
1 litre is slightly more than 1 quart
1 meter is slightly over 3 feet
1 centimeter is approximately 3/8 inch